Starter
Teacher's Booklet

T0352990

Contents

By Lisa Holt

Introduction to Letterland Fix-it Phonics

| Starter | Level 1 | Level 2 | Level 3 |

Age 2-7

Starter - introduces the very **first skills** in language learning.

Level 1 - focuses on **Aa-Zz** shapes and sounds.

Level 2 - revises **a-z** and introduces important **digraphs** (2 letters representing a new sound, e.g **sh** in **sh**op).

Level 3 - introduces more **digraphs**, **trigraphs** and builds the foundations for **full literacy** in English.

Teaching focus and order

The *Fix-it Phonics Starter Level* provides a great foundation in attentive listening skills, a confidence in making sounds and an introduction to basic English vocabulary. *Activity Book 2* includes a first introduction to letter sounds and actions. The teaching order is:

s a t p i n m d g o c k e u r h b f l j v w x y z qu

This recommended order has been chosen for this Starter Level as it matches the order of teaching in *Level 1*. In *Level 1* the order in which sounds are introduced maximises word building possibilities from an early stage.

Alphabet names

You may find that the children in your class already know the traditional alphabet names (**ay, bee, cee...**). They may know an alphabet song, or may have been taught the alphabet names at home. In the early stages of learning, Letterland puts more emphasis on learning the sounds rather than the names simply because when children are learning to read, it is letter sounds rather than alphabet names that help them to read words. You can blend the letter sounds 'mmm...' 'a...' 'nnn...' into the word **man**, but the alphabet names 'em' 'ay' 'en' can only give you a non-word: **emayen**.

Your key to success

At the heart of Letterland teaching are the information-rich pictogram characters.

A pictogram is a visual image that is designed to carry information. Letterland pictograms carry information about each letter's shape and sound. By just starting to say any character's name, children discover the most common sound that letter makes in words.

Letterland pictograms work in accordance with recognised principles of memory and act as mnemonics (memory aids). The result is accelerated letter recognition and quick progress in phonics.

Explain Letterland to your children like this...

When most people look inside a book, all they see are plain, black letters. That's because they haven't been to Letterland and they don't know that every letter is really a Letterland friend.

Letterland is the secret place where all the letters live together. You have been given a special key to unlock that secret place and learn all about the Letterland characters.

Fix-it Phonics
Starter

Resources

Starter resources include:
- ✓ Activity Books 1 and 2 with Stickers
- ✓ Teacher's Booklet with Audio Tracks
- ✓ Animated content on Phonics Online
- ✓ Resource Pack

Activity Books contain:
- ✓ 12 topic-based units
- ✓ teaching notes on every page
- ✓ 16 action songs
- ✓ 26 illustrated action chants
- ✓ a-z letter sounds
- ✓ sticker sheets
- ✓ write-in activities

Audio Access to the *Audio Tracks* is included within this *Teacher's Booklet*. Use every lesson to support your teaching. The *Audio Tracks* include:
- ✓ pronunciation support
- ✓ 26 a-z action chants
- ✓ 16 action songs

Listen along!

Audio Tracks
Scan to listen

Phonics Online contains:
- ✓ 12 topic-based games
- ✓ 12 topic-based songs
- ✓ 16 action songs
- ✓ 26 animated action chants
- ✓ a-z sounds review
- ✓ 7 letter sound games

Resource Pack contains:
✓ 1 board game
✓ 26 action/sound cards
✓ 3 card games
✓ 2 split pin resources

Highly recommended

Action Tricks Poster
Multi-sensory memory clues for the letter sounds are an important component of *Fix-it Phonics Starter* and *Fix-it Phonics Level 1*. Putting this poster on your wall provides a great reference point for the whole class.

Course overview

Fix-it Phonics Starter introduces the very first skills a child needs when starting to learn a language. It provides a great foundation in attentive listening skills, a confidence in making sounds and an introduction to basic English vocabulary.

In this Starter level, children's natural abilities are harnessed as learning is multi-sensory. Children draw, sing, chant, use stickers and do actions - all techniques to make learning fun and memorable.

You can use this programme with children as young as 3 years old. It immerses children in sounds right from the start. The ability to tune into sounds (sound discrimination), remember them (sequencing) and talk about what they have heard (vocabulary and communication skills), is critical in developing children's speaking and listening abilities. Starting with a good foundation makes language learning so much easier.

The course is divided into 7 parts. These include:
- Environmental Sound Discrimination
- Instrumental Sound Discrimination
- Body Percussion and Sound Discrimination
- Rhythm and Rhyme
- Building Oral Language
- Alliteration and Voice Sounds
- Oral Blending

Within these sections, various topics are introduced. The topics are carefully chosen to be the most useful starter oral vocabulary for young learners. Please refer to the Syllabus on pages 8-11 for a full list of topics covered.

Every child will be:
- ✓ involved in making sounds from the very beginning
- ✓ encouraged to listen attentively
- ✓ given plenty of opportunity speak - a real confidence builder for every child
- ✓ encouraged to sing, chant, do actions and use every learning channel
- ✓ play communication games and use English with confidence
- ✓ learn systematically, building oral language and phonological awareness

Making language part of life!

Take it outside!

Fix-it Phonics Starter works as a wonderful classroom-based resource, enabling children to focus on first literacy skills. Learning in an outdoor area can add a real sense of excitement and fun to any lesson. If you have a suitable outdoor space, use it as well!

Encourage children to:

- ✓ listen to the sounds they hear outside
- ✓ use the space outside to make large movements. Swirl ribbons, use sand pits and chalk on the floor to develop the physical skills needed for writing
- ✓ allow children to make sounds with their bodies outside, such as splashing in puddles, tapping objects, marching to a beat or crunching in leaves.

Take it home!

Learning language is all about a good foundation. Even if the parents of your class do not speak English, forming good language learning habits can still be done at home. In the native language parents can instil a love of language by reading to their child, listening out for alliterative sounds, reading rhyming poems and talking about what they see in books. Encourage parents to come and see what you are doing in your *Letterland Fix-it Phonics* classes.

Fix-it Phonics Starter

Syllabus
Activity Book 1

Focus	Topic	Oral language	Songs (Phonics Online)
Environmental Sound Discrimination	Animal noises	Hi. Hello. How are you? I'm fine, thank you. Dog, cat, rat, tiger, monkey, zebra, horse, hen, goat, cow Rhymes: fly/sky, me/sea	Animal noises song
	Outdoor noises	train, car, bike, tractor, scooter, helicopter, plane Rhyming words: cat/sat/mat/rat	Outdoor noises song
Instrumental Sound Discrimination	Numbers 1-6	How old are you? How many? 1-6. Count, clap, stand up, wave, sit down, open your book, close your book	Numbers 1-6 song
	Numbers 1-10	1-10, count, stop	Numbers 1-10 song
	Musical instruments	Drum, fast, slow, loud, quiet, Rhyming words: bell/shell, tree/sea	Musical instruments song
Sound Discrimination & Body Percussion	My feelings	How do you feel? I feel..., happy, sad, tired, angry, scared, laugh, stomp, cry, scream, dad/sad	My feelings song
	My body My face	head, arms, hands, knees, legs, feet, eyes, nose, mouth, jump, turn around Rhyming words: head/bed, hand/sand, knee/tree	My body song
Rhythm and rhyme	Colours	I like... red, yellow, green, orange, blue, pink, rainbow Rhyming words: blue/you	Rainbow colours song
	Shapes	square, triangle, circle, rectangle, oval, star, Rhyming words: where/chair/square	Shapes song

The following skills are introduced throughout *Activity Book 1*

✓attentive listening ✓making noises ✓singing and actions ✓pair work ✓group work ✓role-play ✓syllable clapping ✓rhyming skills ✓observation skills ✓sequencing ✓pencil control skills ✓counting & number skills ✓sound formation with mirrors ✓understanding emotions

Games (Phonics Online)	Resource Pack
Feed the noisy animals! Drag and drop the correct sound.	Animal Sound Pairs
Find the noise. Listen to sounds in sequence.	Transport Pairs
Bang the drum. Listen and repeat. Whistle blowing. Listen and count. 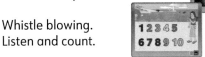	Treasure Hunt board game 
Making music! Listen to sounds in sequence.	Please bring in a selection of real instruments for your class to listen to and play.
Feelings game. Drag and drop.	Feelings Wheel
Build a body. Drag and drop.	It's a boy! It's a girl!
Spot the difference. Visual identification, comparison. Shapes Listen to words in sequence.	Shape Snap

Fix-it Phonics Starter

Syllabus
Activity Book 2

Focus	Topic	Oral language
Building Oral Language	My classroom	This is.. That is... table, chair, window, pencil, pen, book, door, teacher, bag
	My family	mum, dad, sister, brother, grandma, grandpa, family, me, my, love
	My toys	I like...(review) toys, girls, boys, train, ball, car, teddy bear, magic wand, computer game, doll, fairy
	My house	house, welcome, shoes, guide, kitchen, bathroom, sitting room, office, hallway, bedroom
Alliteration & Voice Sounds	**a-z** letter sounds	Letterland character names and actions tricks. New vocabulary in rder of teaching: snake, sun, apple, puppy, ink, insect, nut, milk, duck, dog, goat, on, car, key, kick, egg, elephant, umbrella, up, robot, hat, horse, bed, farm, leg, jet, vet, violin, walrus, wand, yo-yo, zip, zebra, queen, quiet
Oral blending	Sound slide	on, dad, hat, cat, kick, bed, jet, leg, nut, pen, red, six, sun, zip

The following skills are introduced throughout *Activity Book 2*

✓attentive listening ✓making noises ✓singing and actions ✓pair work ✓group work
✓role-play ✓syllable clapping ✓rhyming skills ✓observation skills ✓sequencing ✓pencil control skills
✓counting & number skills ✓sound formation with mirrors ✓alliteration ✓blending sounds

Songs (Phonics Online)	**Games** (Phonics Online)/**Resources**
My classroom song	Find the classroom objects. Drag and drop.
My family song	Find my family! Listen and click.
My toys song	Tidy the toys. Drag and drop.
My house song	Build the house. Drag and drop. *Resource Pack*: Room review
Actions chants Actions song	Action Trick Pairs Game 6 Sound Review Games *Resource Pack* includes 26 Action Trick Cards
Good bye song	Quick Dash Review including word suggestions to blend.

Fix-it Phonics
Starter

Activity Books

The *Activity Books* are designed to be used in the classroom with the *Audio Tracks*. When working with very young children, repetition is very important to consolidate learning. Start and end your lessons in the same way and review oral language as part of your teaching routine.

Lesson Structure - Activity Book 1

Following this simple lesson structure.

Step 1. Start the lesson with the 'Hello' song.

Step 2. Review previous learning with role-play and/or circle time.

Step 3. Introduce a new topic or letter sound. Complete as much as time allows.

Step 4. End each lesson with the 'Good bye' chant and song.

Sing ▶ Listen to the song first. Then join in with just the '**hello**' and '**hi**'. Finally sing the whole song together!

♪ Sing and move!

Hi, hello! Let's wave! Hello.

Hi, hello! Let's wave! Hello.

How are you?

I'm fine, thank you!

Hello, hello. Ok, let's go!

Let's go to Letterland! (x2)

Audio Tracks

The 'Hello' song can be found in the *Audio Tracks* or the Theme Songs Section of *Phonics Online*. The Audio is a **vital** part of this programme. The foundation for building good literacy and language learning skills is the ability to listen well.

Step 1 - Say 'Hello!'

Sing this song at the start of every Letterland lesson to reinforce how to say 'hello' in a memorable, fun and inclusive way.

Encourage the children to stand up, wave, and join in. They may not be able to join in with it all at first, but over time this language will become part of their oral vocabulary.

Phonics Online

Step 2 - Review

Circle Time

Circle Time is just one of the ways you can review the oral language you have taught previously. It ensures that each student gets a chance to contribute and feel valued. The class re-arrange their seating so that they are in a circle facing each other. Or simply sit in a circle on the floor. This means that eye contact is possible at all times making this an inclusive and co-operative activity.

A vital part of language learning is being able to use it with fluency and expression so you can increase the pace in which you go round the circle, or change the style. In *Activity Book 1*, page 42 the instructions **fast**, **slow**, **loud** and **quiet** are introduced, encouraging children to experiment further with sounds.

Choose a child to start. They say 'hello!' (or the review vocabulary). Clockwise each child follows. With each child's turn the aim is to speak faster and faster. Use Circle time repeatedly with the topics listed at beginning of *Activity Book 1*, page 4.

Role-play

At the start of each section, there are also opportunities for the children to consolidate their oral language with pair work and role-play.

You may want to write your own name, and each student's name, on sticky labels. Each child can then put on their label and can begin to recognise their own names.

Step 3 - Introduce a topic

The first skill covered in *Activity Book 1* is Environmental Sound Discrimination. Regardless of the country you live in children will recognise many animal sounds. This first exercise is designed to increase confidence. For the child it is simply an exercise in listening attentively and pointing to the animal they hear.

They then get the opportunity to repeat the exercise making the sounds in pairs.

As they are simply making noises and they are not required to say new English words there is no pressure on the children to 'get it right'. Working with a partner ensures that *all* children are involved in the activity. Participation brings confidence in speaking skills.

Note: Animal noises. The sounds we make to imitate animals can differ. For example, a dog may say 'woof' in one country and 'ruff' in another. It doesn't matter what sound the children use. What is important is that the children work together, confidently make noises and listen to each other.

At the bottom of each page you will find teaching notes. These notes provide explanation and information about the activities on each page so you are aware of the objectives. Remember to read these notes before you complete the exercises with the children so you understand the aim of each page.

This 'listen and point' exercise is repeated to introduce all the different topics in *Activity Books 1* and *2*.

Stickers

As learning language is a complex process, lots of skills have to be mastered. The ability to recognise sounds in sequence is an emergent literacy skill. By doing the sticker activities, your class will be listening attentively, thinking about what they have heard and putting those sounds in order. The use of stickers makes the completion of an activity fun and age appropriate. All children love stickers!

Remember this is not a test. If the children need to listen to the audio again, simply play the track for them so they all experience completing the exercise successfully.

The *Fix-it Phonics Starter* content on *Phonics Online* includes games to consolidate learning. The games are noisy so the children may need to use headphones, or alternatively project the games on a whiteboard and complete them together.

Activity Books

Syllable clapping

Using some type of percussion, such as clapping hands, drums, rhythm sticks, maracas, etc., the children learn to tap out each syllable in the word. This is another emergent literacy skill.

Children can't begin to understand how English may be written down, unless they can understand that it is made up of multiple parts. As a first step, we listen out for syllables within a word before moving on to individual phonemes.

Some children may be able to do this well while others may not fully understand what they are listening for. Model the concept clearly with a word they all know, such as 'Hello' (2 syllables).

Clap — Listen to the words. Then listen as the drum plays for each syllable in the word. You try clapping or drumming the syllables.

Drum or clap!

| dog | cat | rat |

| tiger | monkey | zebra |

Syllable clapping — Being able to identify syllables allows children to begin to associate spoken language with written words.

9

Rhyming skills

There has been a significant quantity of research that indicates the correlation between rhyming mastery and eventual reading preparedness.

Encourage children to come up with rhymes in their native language, so you are sure they fully understand what a 'rhyme' is.

Rhyme time is repeated throughout the *Activity Books*.

Children enjoy rhymes because rhymes play with language and children love all forms of play.

Rhyming skills are revisited in *Fix-it Phonics - Level 1*. At this stage it does not matter if your class does not understand *every* word. The aim is to begin to recognise rhyming words.

Later on you will find that understanding how rhymes work gives children a happy start in reading and spelling simple words.
A child who can read and spell 'cat' will be more likely to be able to read and spell 'mat', 'rat' and 'sat'.

Sing and move!

The action songs provide a playful way to help children develop their vocabularies and awareness of sounds. Young children love to get their whole body involved in learning rather than sit down at a table to learn. These songs allow the children to stand up, move about and release all the energy they inevitably have. At the same time as consolidating any new vocabulary, they will be learning balance coordination, body awareness and rhythm. The songs start off very simple - the Animal song is mostly noises. Gradually, over the course of the level, more complex language is introduced.

The software provides an engaging alternative to the *Audio Tracks*. You could have a 'Songs session' in which you review all the songs together.

Hello, cat. Miaow! Miaow!

Rainbow, rainbow. Red and yellow.

Activity Books

Write-in sections

The *Activity Books* can be used in class, or you can set specific exercises for children to complete at home with their parents. Next to each exercise you will see a tab showing the learning skill.

Drawing and colouring pictures is an important part of learning. Children develop the pencil control they need for writing by focusing on keeping the colour within specified areas. Encourage them to talk about the colours they are choosing, too.

There are various types of activities in this section including:

- Patterns & sequencing
- Visual discrimination
- Looking and thinking
- Pencil control

The correct handwriting position.

It would be a good idea to spend time ensuring every child adopts a good handwriting position before starting this book.

Right-hander

Paper side edge
20°
Table edge

Chair slightly tilted
Feet on floor

Finger tips 2 cm
from tip of pencil

Left-hander

Paper side edge
30°
Table edge

Elbows off the table
Feet on floor

Finger tips 4 cm
from tip of pencil

Step 4 - Say 'Good Bye'

In the same way that starting a lesson with a 'Hello' song is important, finishing the session is equally important too. Encourage the children to stand up, wave, and join in. The words are simple and useful. Over time this language will become part of their oral vocabulary. The song is available on the accompanying audio.

Let's check!

You will notice that at the end of each part there is a listening exercise. You can use these to assess an individual's ability, or let the children work more informally in groups or pairs.

It is important that children don't feel intimidated by these exercises. Complete the first few questions together as a group, so you can be sure that each child understands what they are expected to do.

You may continue to do this as a group exercise rather than individual assessment.

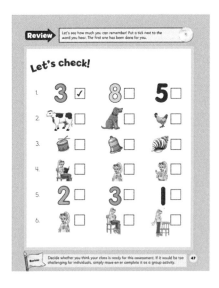

Activity Book 2
Part 6 - Alliteration & Voice Sounds

In *Activity Book 2*, Part 6, alphabet sounds and actions are introduced. At this stage, emphasis should be on having fun whilst introducing the basic concept of associating letter shapes with sounds. The teaching order is:

s a t p i n m d g o c k e u r h b f l j v w x y z q

This recommended teaching order maximises word building possibilities from an early stage in *Level 1*.

Part 6 Actions help to develop multi-sensory memory clues for the letter sounds. Start the sessions by singing the song which starts, '**Now it's time to do actions!**' This song is lively and should really get the children wide awake and ready to learn each new Letterland character, letter sound and action.

Actions and chants

Do the action as you listen to the chant. Simple instructions for each action are included in the teaching notes at the bottom of the page. There are also animated actions for each letter on *Phonics Online*. Furthermore, there is a poster of all the actions is available for your wall.
(See resources - *Action Tricks Poster*).

Listen to the rhythm of the chant, too. Rhythm is an integral part of speech so developing an awareness of rhythm at an early stage is an invaluable language skill.

Part 6 - Alliteration & Voice Sounds

The write-in pages relating to the Letterlanders include an introduction to alliterative vocabulary. The Letterland names themselves are alliterative and embedded in the character names are many useful vocabulary building words.

Encourage children to look at the pictures on the page and say the words out loud. They can then colour the picture trying to keep the colour within the specified areas. At this stage you are not expecting the children to start writing the letter shapes. Some children may naturally want to have a go, while others may be very reluctant to even hold a pencil. Formation of letter shapes is covered in *Fix-it Phonics Level 1*, so the aim of these exercises is more to familiarise children with the visual images so they start to recognise each shape and associate it with the correct sound and action.

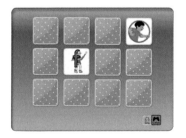

When all **a-z** actions have been introduced, you may want to play the 'Pairs' game on *Phonics Online* which further reinforces the link between each Letterland character and its action and sound.

On completing the introduction of all the letter sounds and actions, learn the Action Song (p. 84-86, *Activity Book 2*).

This is a full alphabet review. A sing-along version is available to project onto a whiteboard on *Phonics Online*. Learning this song will be quite a challenge, and revisiting it many times, even throughout teaching of *Fix-it Phonics Level 1*, will be of real benefit to the children. You can be assured that the challenge will be engaging, and once mastered, the children will have really conquered the letter shape/sound association.

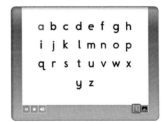

The *Resource Pack* contains 26 Action Cards. The Letterland characters are on one side and the Action Tricks are on the reverse side. You can use these cards to review all the **a-z** letter sounds and actions. You could also play games with the cards.

For example, one child could come to the front and pick a card, then do the action to the class. The class has to guess the correct letter sound.

Part 7 - Oral blending

In Part 7, the concept of blending sounds together to form words is introduced. This is an **oral exercise** so there are just a few pages of visuals to look at in the *Activity Books* (pages 80-83).

Only start to try and blend sounds together if you feel your class is ready. At this stage it does not matter if children are unable to blend or segment the sounds themselves. All letter sounds are introduced in greater detail and blending techniques are consolidated in *Fix-it Phonics Level 1*.

The aim of this section is to enable children to start to *see* and *hear* that words are made up of separate phonemes.

The Sound Slide

If you are familiar with Letterland teaching techniques, you may have already come across the popular 'Roller Coaster Trick'. In this programme we have adapted the trick for younger children who may not be familiar with what a roller coaster is. Most children will know what a slide is though!

The Sound Slide allows them to 'see' and 'feel' the sounds as they blend together to make the words. The child needs to think of their arm as a slide with the sounds attached. Slide down to blend the sounds. This technique helps children imagine the sounds in order. Say the individual sounds first, then move faster down your arm slide to blend the sounds!

Gradually introduce more words. Use only 1-syllable words and make sure that they are easily 'sounded out'. Start off with three-letter words only, but as children grow in confidence you can introduce blending four sounds together. There is a list of words on page 83 of *Activity Book 2*. This list is vocabulary the children should already be familiar with.

More decodable words (those that can easily be 'sounded out') can be found in the *Phonics Online* 'Cards Tool'. Introduce and explain as much of this vocabulary as you feel is appropriate for your class.

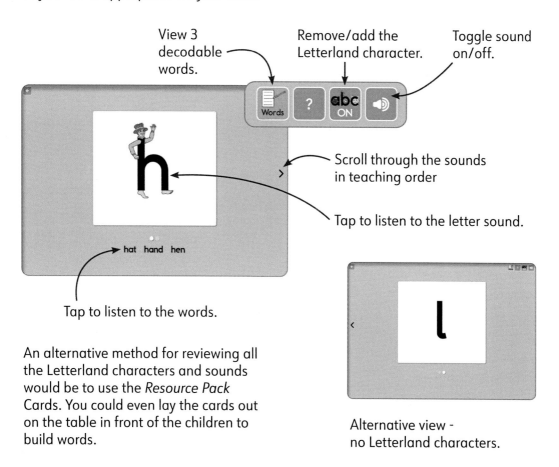

View 3 decodable words.

Remove/add the Letterland character.

Toggle sound on/off.

Scroll through the sounds in teaching order

Tap to listen to the letter sound.

hat hand hen

Tap to listen to the words.

Alternative view - no Letterland characters.

An alternative method for reviewing all the Letterland characters and sounds would be to use the *Resource Pack* Cards. You could even lay the cards out on the table in front of the children to build words.

Software

The software (available on *Phonics Online*) is designed to accompany the *Activity Books* and *Audio Tracks*. When children are very young, sitting at desks and looking at books can only be done for short periods of time. Children love to stand up, move about, release energy and get their whole bodies participating in activities. They love to play games, press buttons, hear noises and get instantaneous feedback. We understand that every classroom is different in the early years setting. Some will have multiple computers, some will have one that they can project onto a whiteboard, others will not have any at all. The *Activity Books* include icons and suggestions when it would be useful to play a game or look at a song on the software. How and when you use it has to be dependent upon your individual teaching circumstances.

Songs

The *Starter* programme relies heavily on audio work and multi-sensory action songs and chants. To further engage the children, all the songs on *Phonics Online* are animated. To watch the simple actions on screen before joining in helps to ensure that everyone understands the actions and meaning of the songs.

Games

A selections of games, detailed in the syllabus on pages 8-11 are included. The focus of this programme is improving listening skills and sound discrimination. For that reason you will find that many of the games are noisy! If you are using the software on multiple computers it may be a good idea to provide headphones for the children as well.

Actions

As described on page 19 of this booklet, the **a-z** action chants are animated. There is also a 'pairs' game for children to practise matching the action to the correct Letterlander.

Sounds

There are two ways to review all of the letter sounds. The first, 'Cards Tool', is described on page 23. The second is a series of games which scroll through in order of learning. You will find these games as you work through the sounds in the 'Meet the Letterlanders' section of *Phonics Online*. These games require the user to listen to a series of sounds and select the correct characters in order. If they fail to get the sequence correct, they must start again. If they complete the task, a new game begins.

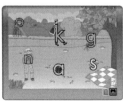

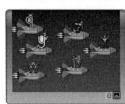

Resource Pack

The *Resource Pack* contains detailed instructions on how to play each game and make best use of the resources. When and how often you use the games is entirely discretionary.

Some of the resources, such as the *Feelings Wheel* and *Room Review* can be shown to the whole class to refresh memories, while others, such as the *Pairs* game are best played with 2-3 children only.

When you have completed *Activity Book 1*, you may want to have a 'Games session'. Set up six stations (tables or areas) each with a different game. Let the children play the game at a station for a selected amount of time (7-10 mins) then ask them to change stations. Rotate the class around the different stations as often as time allows.

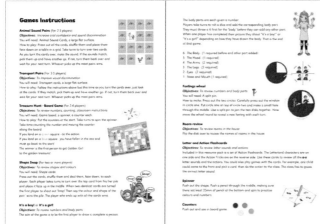

The resources could also be reserved for those children working at a faster pace than others. They could act as an incentive or reward for finishing other work.

Encourage children to use as much of their English as possible when playing the games. If the game involves a spinner or dice, remind the children to read the number in English, or count in English as they move along the board in a board game. The *Action Trick Cards* are a particularly useful resource to review letter sounds and actions (as described on page 23). This resource will continue to be useful when you move on to *Fix-it Phonics Level 1*.

Next steps

When you have completed *Activity Book 2*, be sure to award each child with their own certificate. Certificates are a great way to motivate children and give them a sense of accomplishment.

After completing *Fix-it Phonics Starter*, move on to *Fix-it Phonics Level 1*.

Level 1 moves on to introduce:

- letter recognition skills - sounds & shapes (Aa-Zz + long vowels)
- listening and speaking skills
- basic English vocabulary
- oral blending and segmenting
- high-frequency words.

Creative ideas

Playing with sounds and encouraging children to become attentive listeners can be a lot of fun. Below are a few more suggestions for getting your class involved.

Make shakers. Use plastic bottles and fill them with different materials, such as sand, pebbles, rice or coins. If they are nontransparent bottles you can then ask the children to listen carefully and describe what might be in the bottles. Shakers can be used again in listening and joining in with the beat of music.

Sound collections. Use a recording device and collect 'favourite' sounds. You could even make a song of favourite sounds.

Sound matching. The sound a musical instrument can make can have a personality! Play different types of music (classical / jazz / pop) and ask the children to match them to a particular animal. For example, a deep, plodding piece of music involving tubas may sound like an elephant, whereas a high pitched fast, scurrying music (violins/ keyboard) may represent a mouse well. It is fine for the children to use their native language to describe the sounds as this will still allow them to hone their listening skills and in the long term this will enable them to become better language learners.

Alliterative creatures. To play with alliteration, before children have a large English vocabulary, remember you can use nonsense words.

Make up some weird and wonderful creatures, such as a: **be boppy bang**, or a **tungle tapper tee**. These are imaginary creatures using imaginary words, but the children are still strengthening skills in alliteration and sound awareness.

Sounds box. As the children learn more English vocabulary, you could create a box to collect objects/flashcards that begin with the same sound. Emphasise the initial sound as they go in the box.

First interest in letter shapes

Fix-it Phonics Starter focuses primarily on getting children ready orally for learning language. Having good pencil control and being able to form letters usually comes later in development. However, some children may have a lot of interest in the letter shapes themselves. Below are a few suggestions to foster this interest.

Draw patterns. Show how to draw patterns, using different colours to make it fun. Zigzags, arches, straight lines and circles will all be used later for making letter shapes, so they are good ways to start learning pencil control and letter formation.

Model the letters. You could begin with play dough for fun. Make the letters and then add animating details in different colours.

Vary the tools. Provide different things to write with on different days, such as – pens, coloured pencils, chalks or thick tipped markers. Add variety with a wet paint brush, or a stick to write with in sand. You could even use a tray of flour, rice, lentils, or shaving cream to finger trace the letters in. You may also have access to a drawing app on a computer, tablet or smartphone – for practising all those shapes.

Make display places. Display the children's pictures on the wall or notice board, so they can see that you value their work.

Use old newspapers or magazines. Look in magazines, books and signs for letters they have just learned. If possible, circle them with a red marker pen.

Costumes & Props

Children love to dress up, especially as their favourite Letterland characters. It strengthens their emotional bonds with the letters and sounds and helps build very positive expectations of the learning experience. You may want to make/collect items so your class can 'become' Letterlanders!

Learning objectives

When children are very young formal assessment is not really required. However, it is useful to remember the learning objectives while teaching to ensure children develop a great foundation in speaking and listening skills.

The course is divided into 7 parts. These include:
- Environmental Sound Discrimination
- Instrumental Sound Discrimination
- Body Percussion and Sound Discrimination
- Rhythm and Rhyme
- Building Oral Language
- Alliteration and Voice Sounds
- Oral Blending

By the end of this course, your objectives are to have a group of children who can:

Check

☐ listen attentively;

☐ speak confidently to adults and other children;

☐ have an increased English vocabulary;

☐ discriminate phonemes;

☐ reproduce audibly phonemes they hear, in order, through a word;

☐ use the Sound Slide to blend phonemes together.